the·world·at·your·feet

BUILD YOUR OWN
EMPIRE STATE BUILDING

A PERIGEE BOOK
ALAN ROSE

Perigee Books
are published by
G. P. Putnam's Sons
200 Madison Avenue
New York, New York 10016

Copyright © 1980 by Alan Rose
All rights reserved. This book, or parts thereof, may
not be reproduced in any form without permission.
ISBN 0-399-50506-7
First Perigee Printing, 1980
Printed in the United States of America
Third Impression

THE EMPIRE STATE BUILDING

FOR HUNDREDS OF MILLIONS of people around the world, the Empire State Building is more than just another gray skyscraper rising above the commercial hub of America. For them, it is America itself, an architectural cliché of such enduring power that it at once symbolizes both the economic and technical prowess of the greatest city in a great nation and is emblematic of the raw dynamicism of the twentieth century. From Kinshasa to Copenhagen and from Djakarta to Des Moines, the Empire State Building is exactly what its developer promised it would be: the Eighth Wonder of the World.

Two hundred years ago the plot of land that stands where Fifth Avenue and Thirty-fourth Street now converge was a grassy meadow, a two-acre chunk of John Thompson's farm, which, in Thompson's words, comprised "a new and convenient house, barn and several out-houses. . . . The land is fertile, partly wooded and well-watered and eminently suitable for the raising of various produce, profitably disposed of to the opulent families of the City. . . ." John Thompson's twenty-acre farm was valued at less than $10,000 in 1825. But by 1827, only two years later, the property was worth twice that amount. It was sold to William Backhouse Astor, the second son of John Jacob, for some $20,000. For nearly six decades, the Astors lived in splendor at Fifth and Thirty-fourth, entertaining their friends from New York's fabled "400"—the city's moneyed aristocracy—in houses that cost millions to build. But by the 1890s, the Astors had tired of life in Manhattan and relocated elsewhere. William Waldorf Astor determined that New York City badly needed a grand hotel, one that would reflect proudly the city's new status, so on Monday, March 13, 1893, he opened the Waldorf-Astoria.

The hotel was a monument to Victorian excess. Built at a cost of $5 million, the Waldorf sported elegant private dining rooms, spacious ballrooms, and enormous salons filled with the Astor family's surplus furniture and service. It was the centerpiece of New York society.

In 1928, Alfred E. Smith, four times governor of New York and a candidate for President that year, organized a group of businessmen who wished to erect an office building of monumental proportions. As announced in The New York *Times,* the edifice was to contain "eighty stories . . . and will cost, with the sixteen million paid for the site, more than sixty million dollars." In 1929, the deal was consummated, and, as the nation's economy began disintegrating, architect William Frederick Lamb began drawing his plans. Late that year, the Waldorf was demolished; by spring, 1930, the structural steel of the new building was rising; and by the summer of that year, the external masonry was being applied.

But 1930 was also the year that Walter Chrysler unveiled his new building: the Chrysler Building. At 1,046 feet, the Chrysler Building was 62 feet higher than the Eiffel Tower, and hence, the tallest building in the world.

Undeterred, the Smith group pressed ahead with construction. Additional floors were added, and, finally, a tower for mooring dirigibles was conceived. More than three thousand men worked on the building every day, and on May 1, 1931, the Empire State Building, now some 102 stories high and with its dirigible mast expanded into an observation tower soaring 1,250 feet over Fifth Avenue, opened its doors to an awestruck city when President Hoover threw the switch that illuminated the building.

The world's tallest building, however, still had its share of troubles ahead of it. Even as the "Eighth Wonder of the World" reached to the sky over Manhattan, the nation was plunging deeper into economic depression. For much of the 1930s, the Empire State Building was less than half occupied; by the outbreak of the second world war, occupancy was on the rise, but in 1945 another disaster struck—literally out of the blue. A Mitchell B-25 bomber smashed into the 79th floor. Fourteen people, including the plane's three-man crew, died in the accident, and dozens more were injured. Damage to the building was estimated at more than a million dollars.

After the war, the Empire State Building began reaping the rewards that its developers had projected. But by the 1960s, newer skyscrapers were encroaching on its record. In 1950, it was decided that a 22-story, 222-foot, 60-ton radio and television antenna would be mounted atop the building. With the new antenna, the building reached 1,472 feet. Its record was safe for several more years until the opening of the World Trade Center in Lower Manhattan.

While it may have lost its title of the world's tallest building, the Empire State Building continues to rise above its competitors in stature and history. In many ways it is still what Alfred E. Smith proclaimed it to be more than half a century ago: The Eighth Wonder of the World.

The original Waldorf-Astoria Hotel

The Empire State Building at night.
UNITED PRESS PHOTO BY STAFF PHOTOGRAPHER ANDREW LOPEZ

GENERAL INSTRUCTIONS

WHAT YOU NEED TO BUILD THE EMPIRE STATE BUILDING: Glue, scissors, and about eight hours. That's it. Any of the following items, however, might come in handy: masking tape, a metal-edged ruler, a single-edge razor blade (or an X-acto knife with #11 blade), an ice cream stick, and a toothpick. If you have these things around the house, that's fine; if not, don't worry. None of them are worth a special trip.

TIPS BEFORE BEGINNING

Gluing: A white transparent glue, such as Elmer's, is best. Use glue sparingly, but be sure to cover the entire surface of each tab so that edges joined together stay together. Before you glue a piece in place, check its alignment with the assembly drawing, then apply the glue to the tab surface. A toothpick is useful for reaching difficult areas, and an ice cream stick can be used to wipe off excess glue. Or you can use your fingers. Be sure to allow sufficient time for drying before handling.

Scoring: Most pieces in this book require crisp, neat edges. To make a crease in the paper so that folds can be made sharply, use a ball-point pen, the edge of a scissors, or a pencil. If you use an X-acto or razor blade for scoring, use the dull edge or a light touch. If you make a mistake and cut through a piece while scoring, the damage can be repaired with tape. *Score exactly on the score marks provided and score each piece before cutting it out.* Reverse scores can be made by lining up a ruler along the score mark and puncturing the paper at the top and bottom of the mark, using the edge of an X-acto. Then turn the sheet over, use the ruler to line up the two marks, and make the score line. Don't punch a hole in the printed surface of the part. And don't make the mistake of cutting on a line that indicates a score. Examine the key to symbols carefully.

Tape: Masking tape can be used to hold together parts while the glue is drying. But test the tape first on the surface of the paper to make sure it won't damage the printed surface when removed.

Cutting: Each piece should be carefully removed, with as much of the black cut-lines removed as possible.

ASSEMBLY INSTRUCTIONS

The first thing to do is to make this book look like something other than a book. Ultimately, it will look like the Empire State Building, but for now it should look like a stack of loose sheets. So remove the staples without tearing the pages and pull the loose sheets apart. Score each piece on each sheet before cutting (except for piece G6). Each piece is coded with a letter and a color. Cut each piece out of the sheet and group it with other pieces of the same letter-color code. Examine the drawings before starting each assembly section. After cutting each piece, fold along score lines.

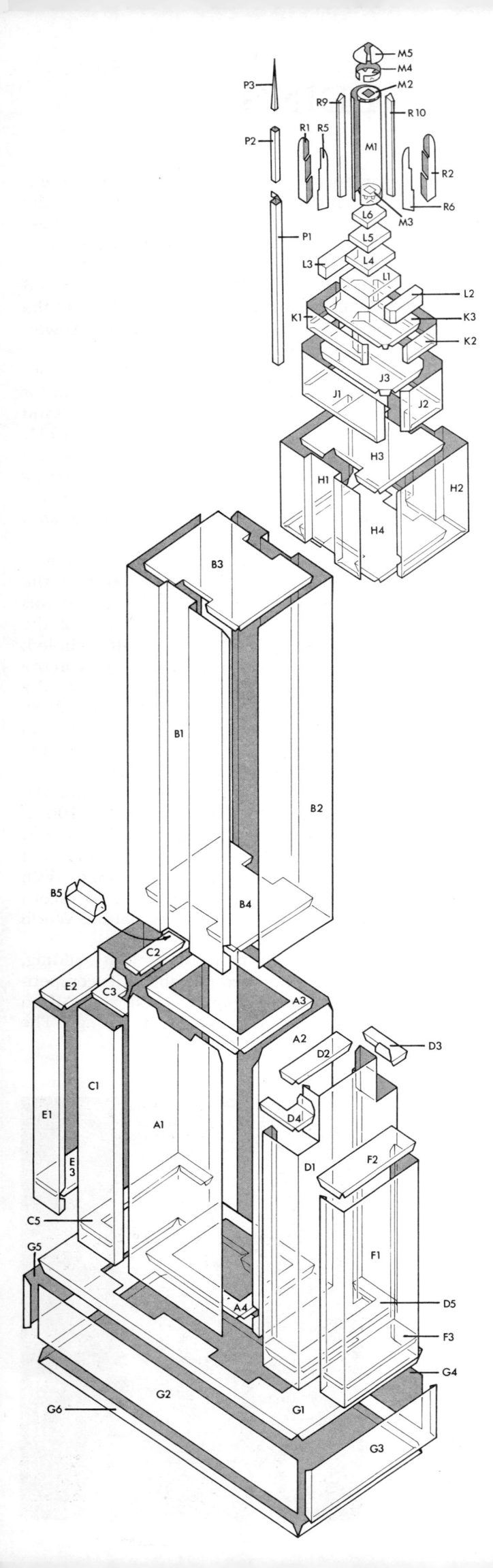

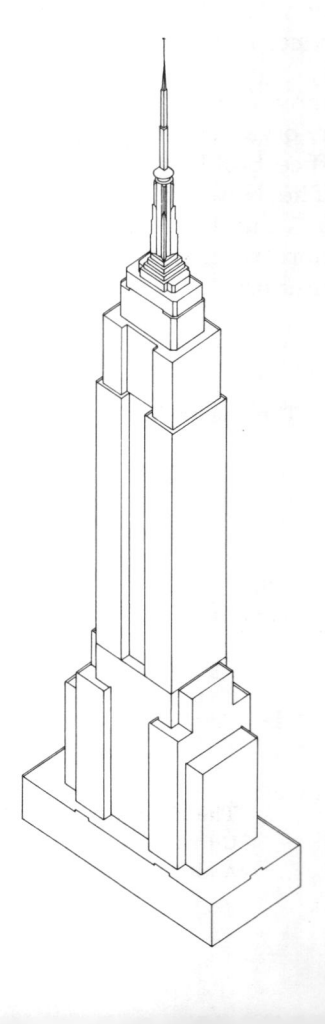

B2

B1

A1

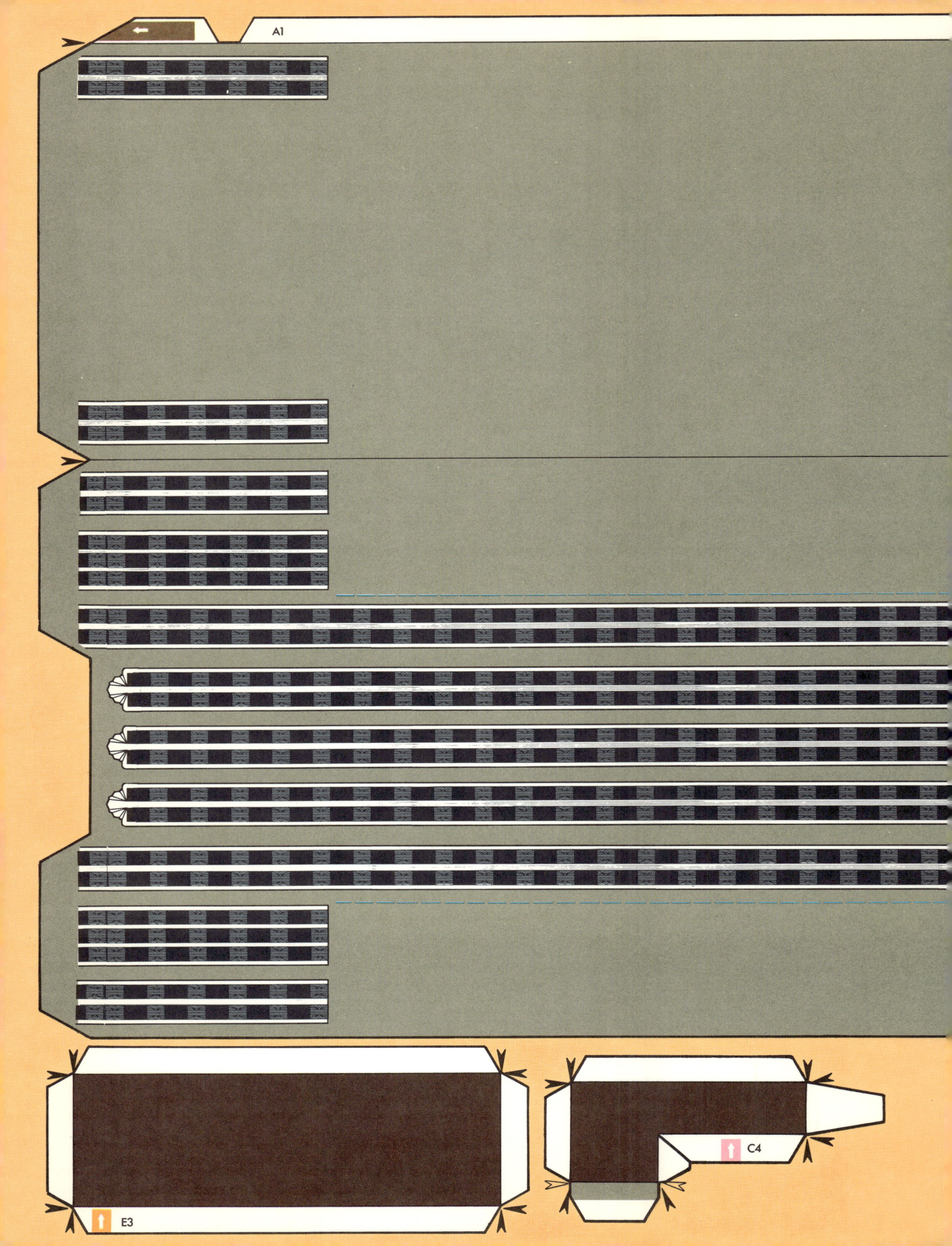

C4

E3

EXTRA R5 R7

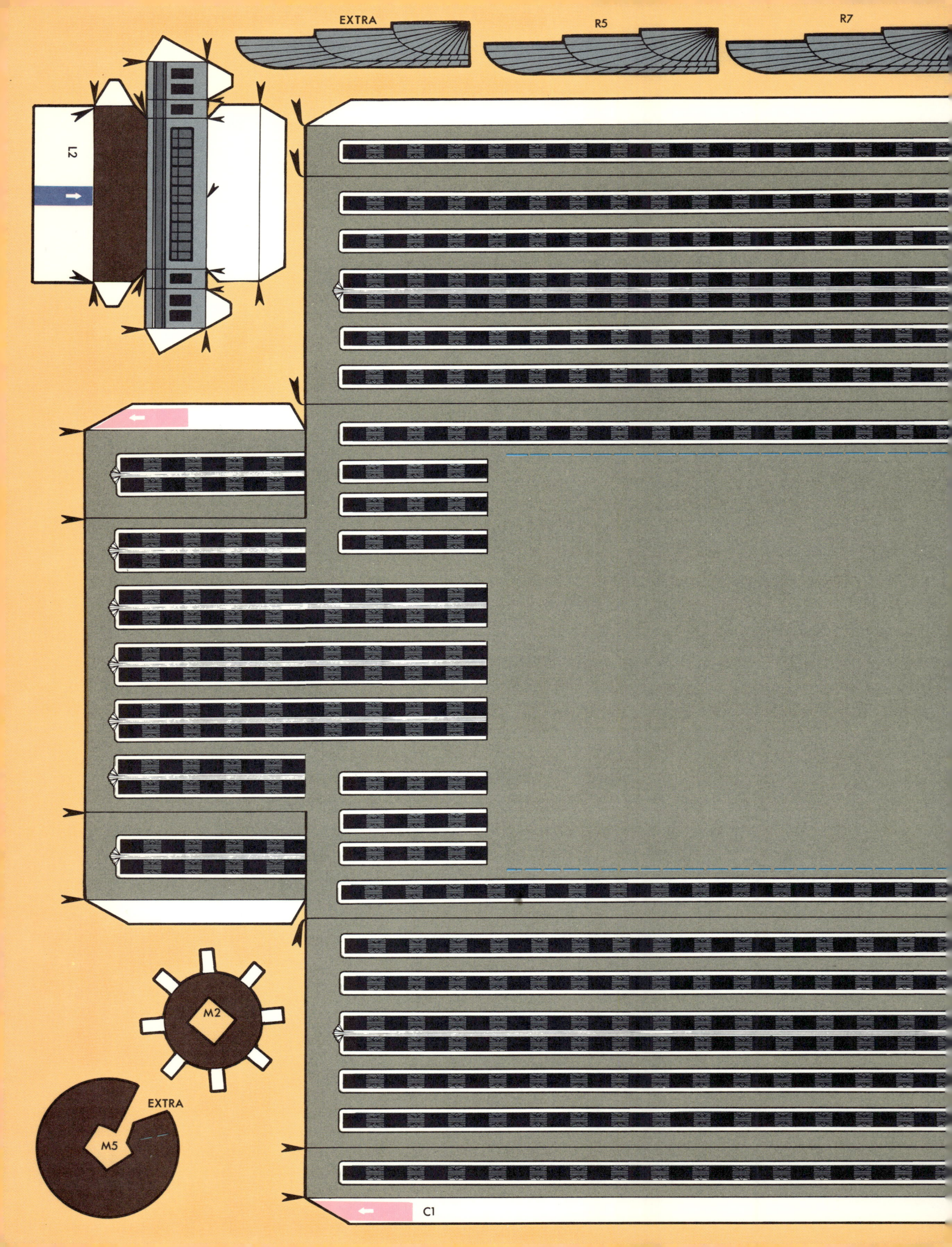

L2

C1

M2

EXTRA
M5

© 1980 ALAN ROSE

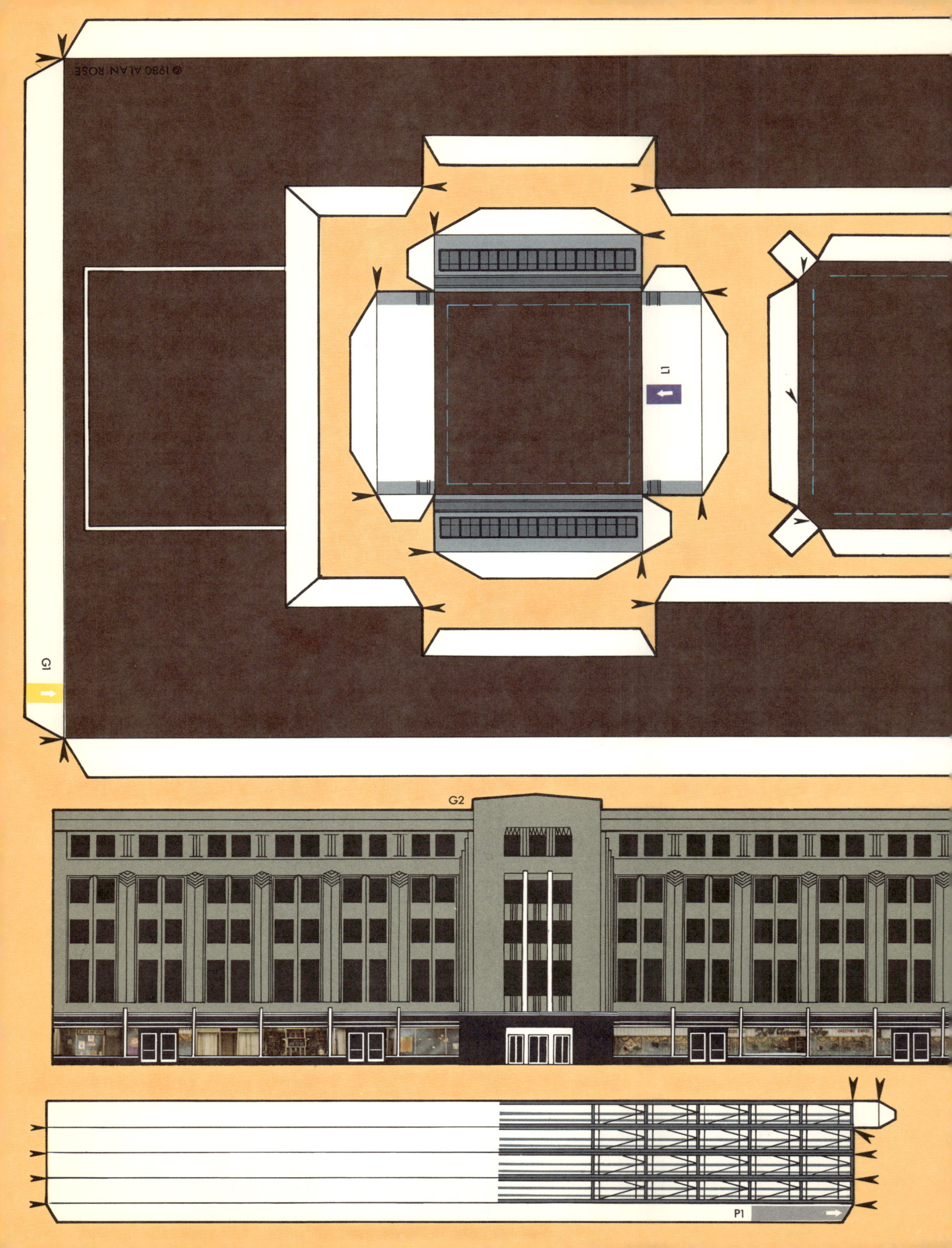

G1

L1

G2

P1

A2

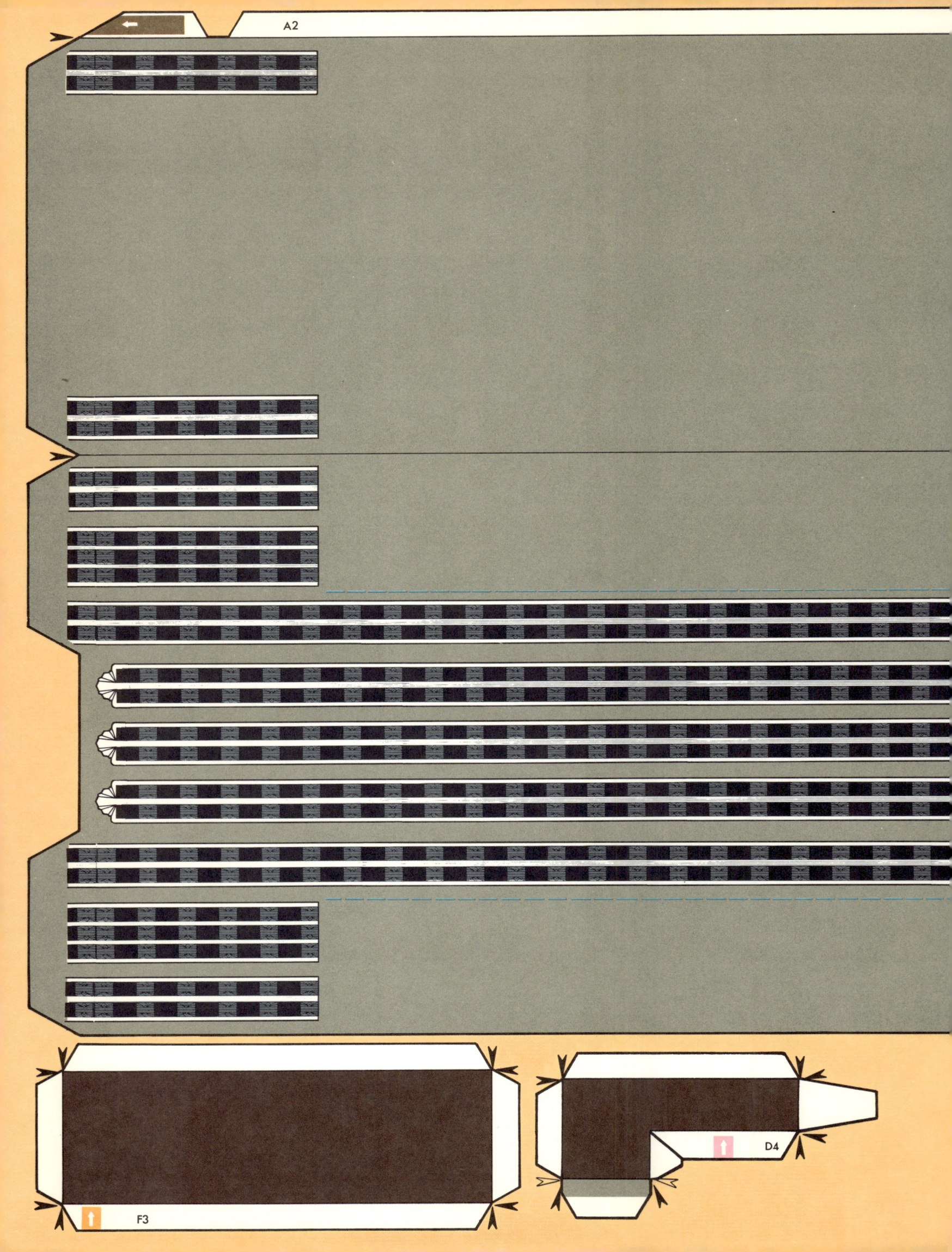

F3

D4

EXTRA R6 R8

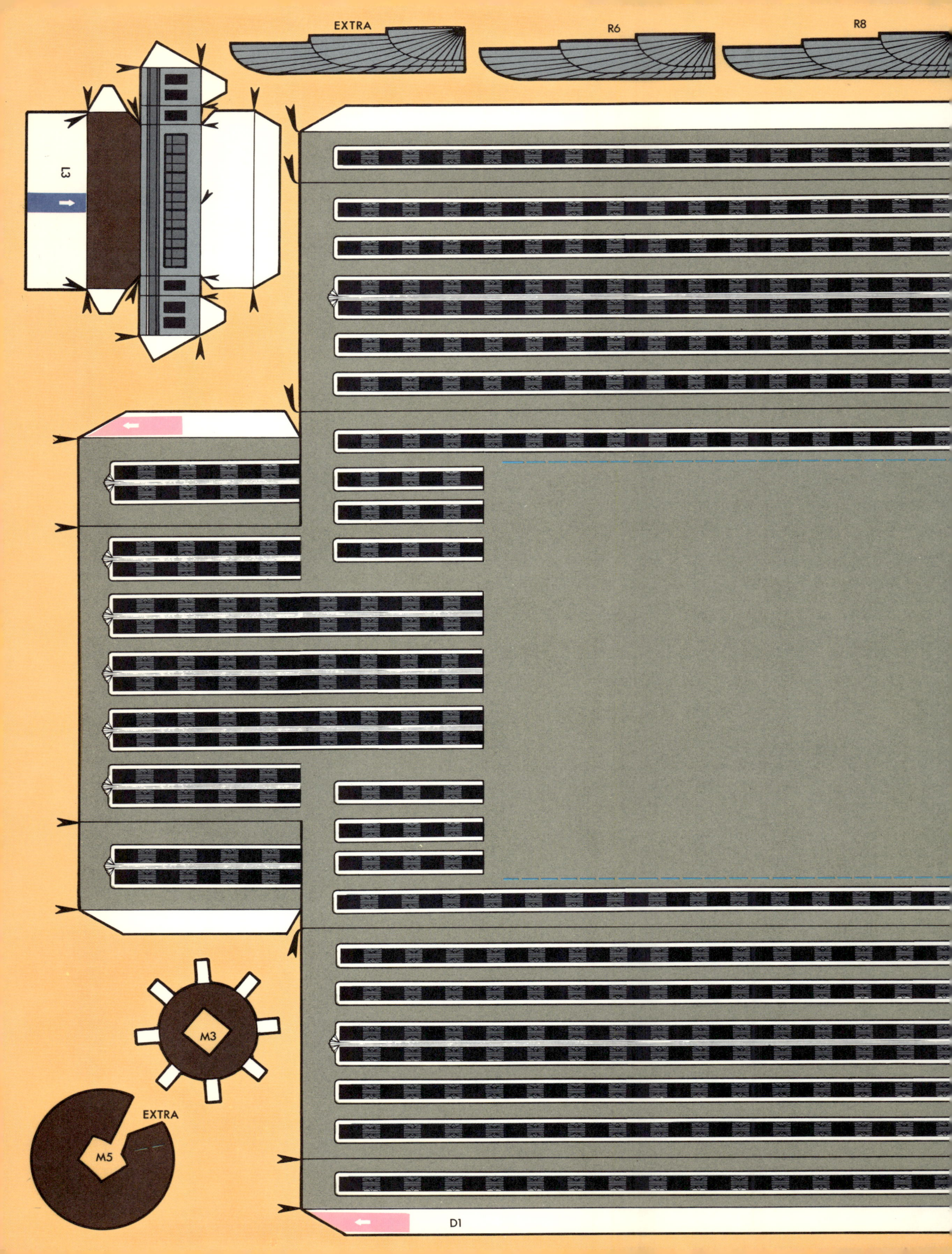

L3

M3

EXTRA
M5

D1

E1

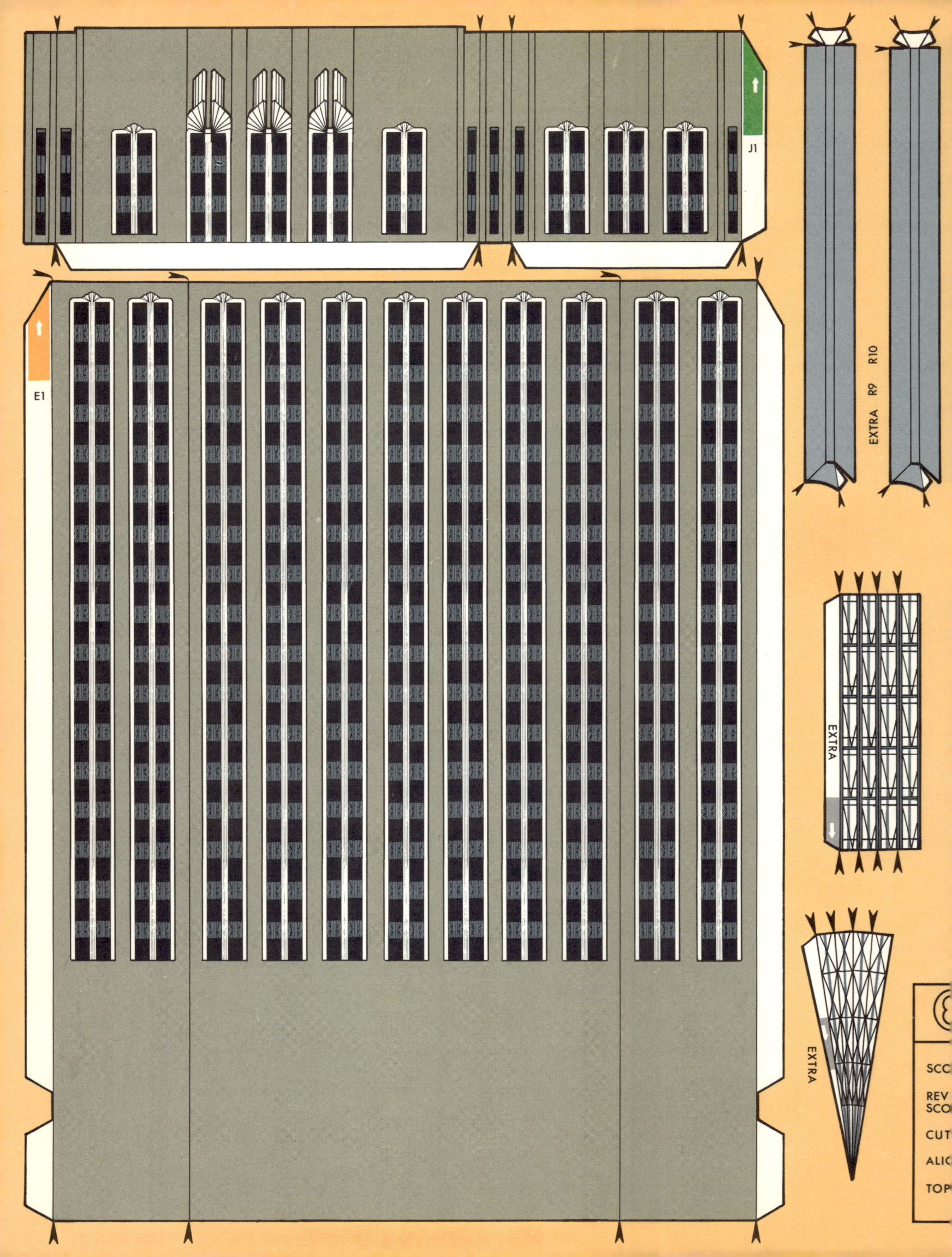

J1

EXTRA R9 R10

EXTRA

EXTRA

SCO
REV SCO
CUT
ALIG
TOP

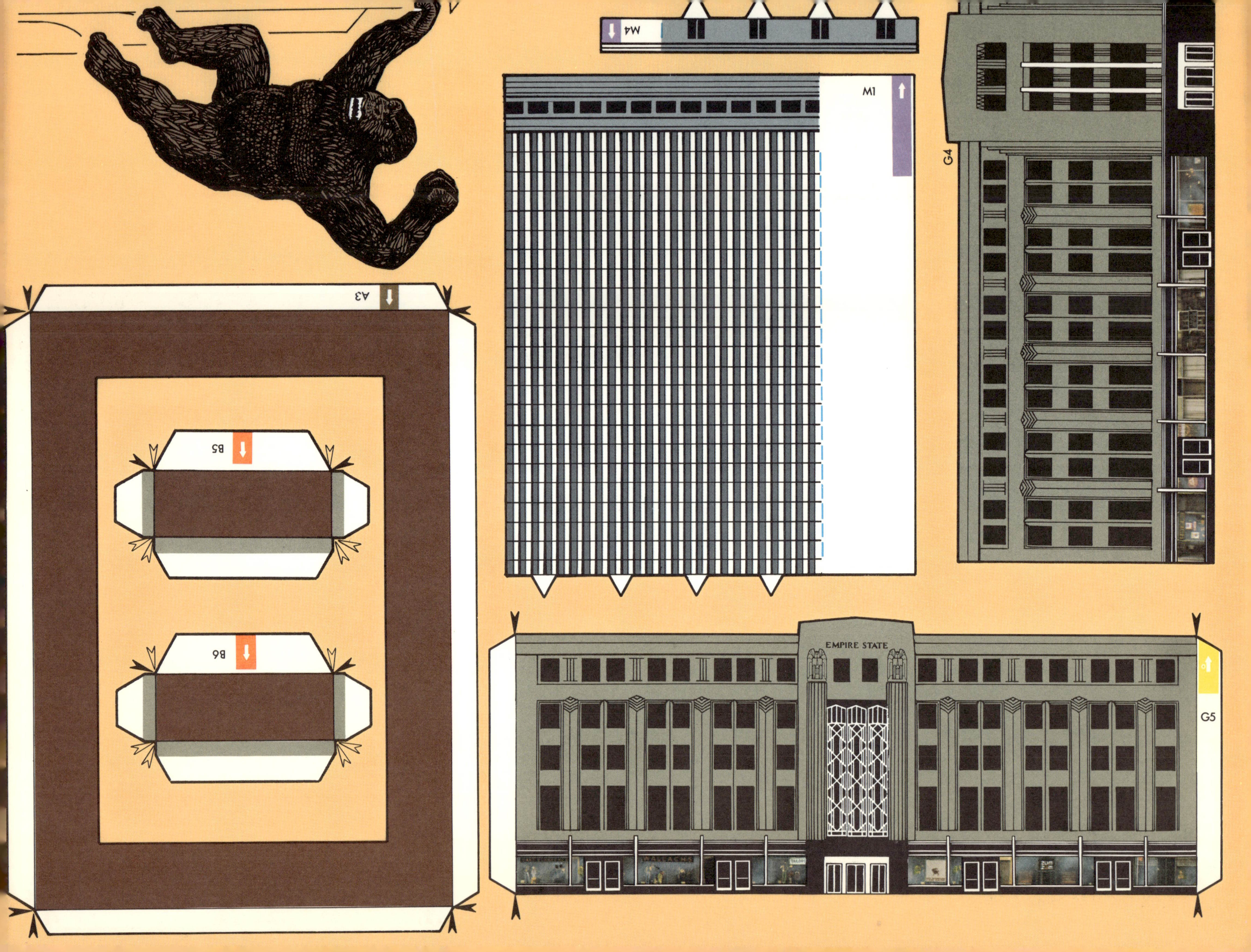

A3
B5
B6
M1
M4
G4
G5
EMPIRE STATE

J4

H3

L4

L5

L6

C6

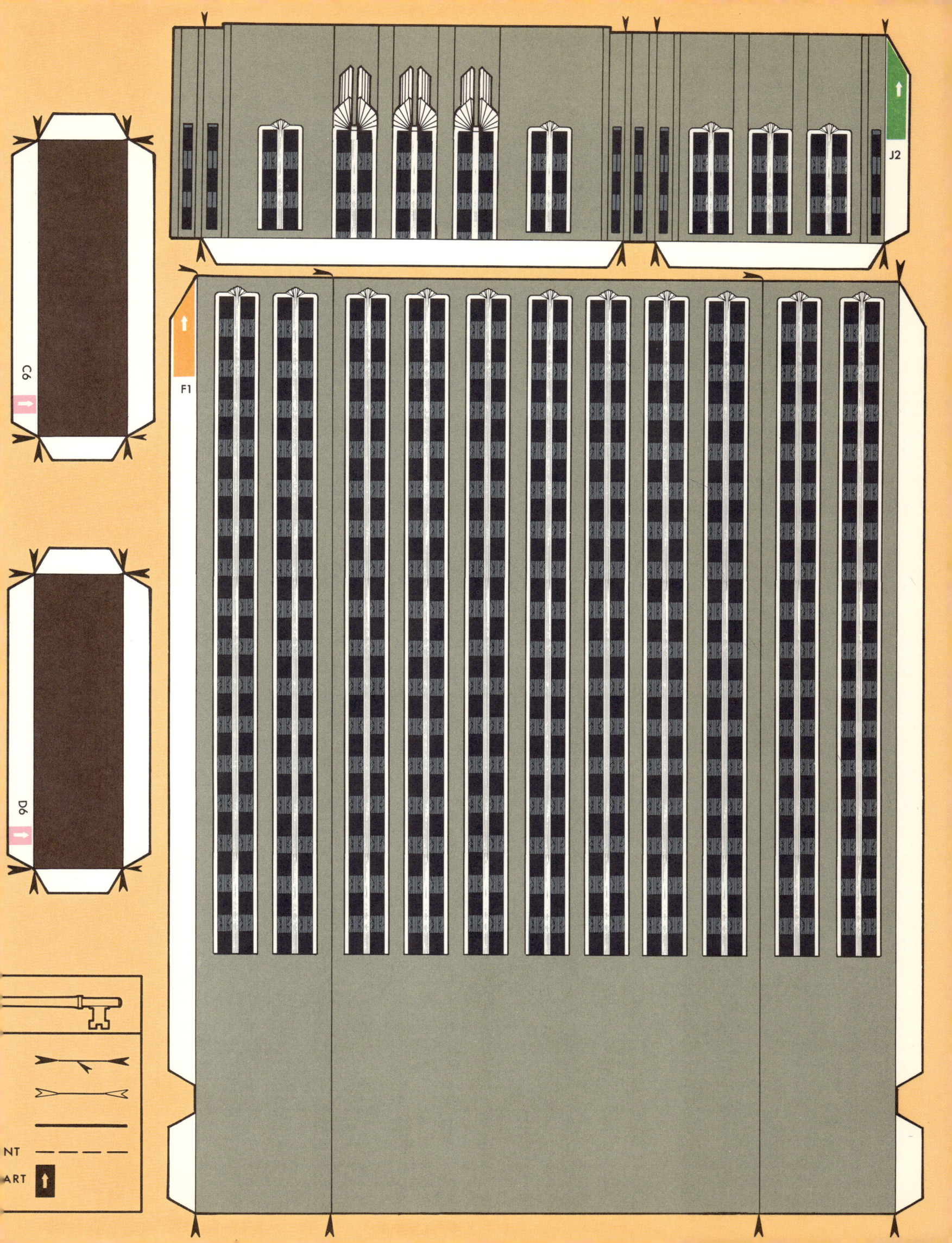

D6

F1

J2

NT
ART

EXTRA

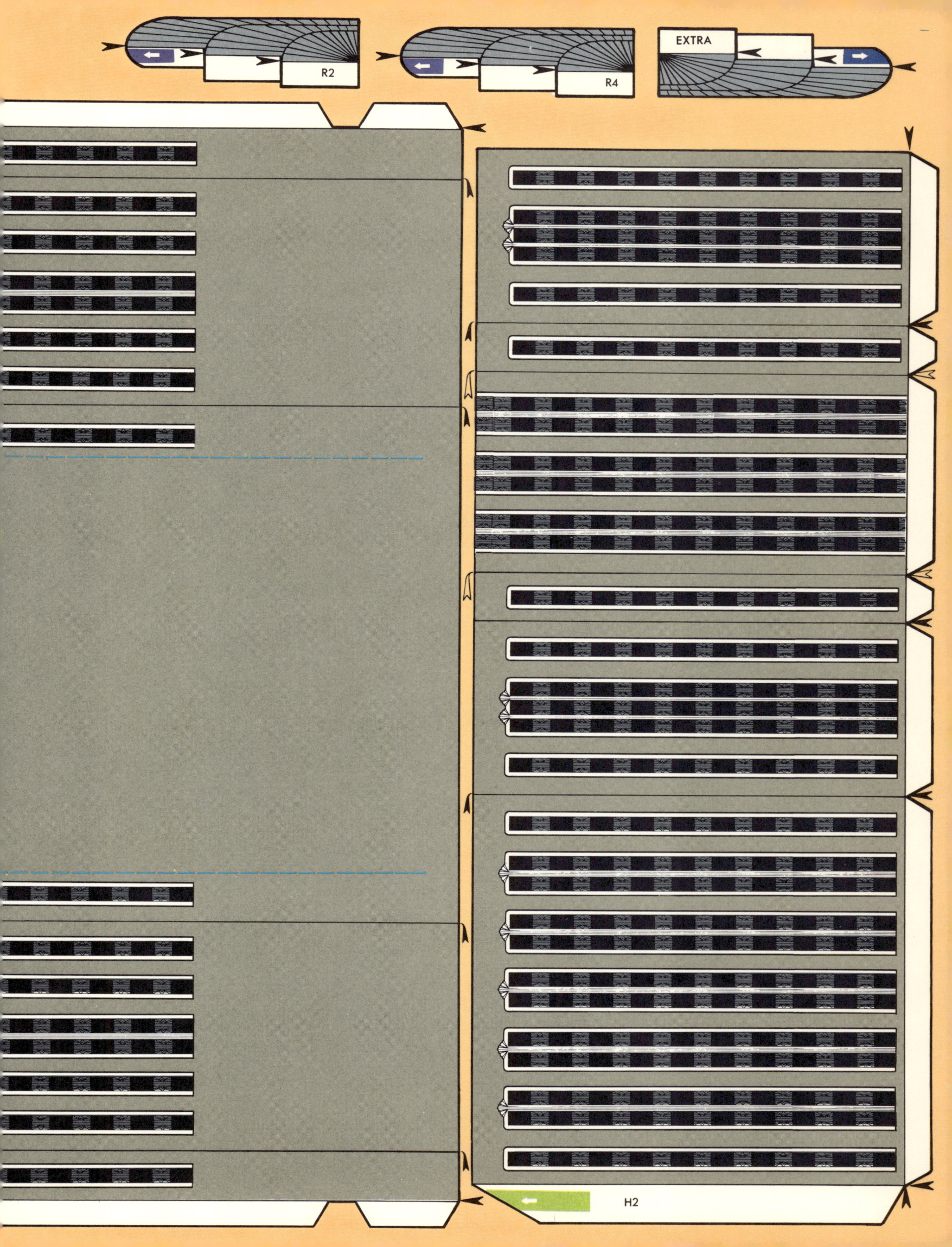

R2

R4

H2

B4

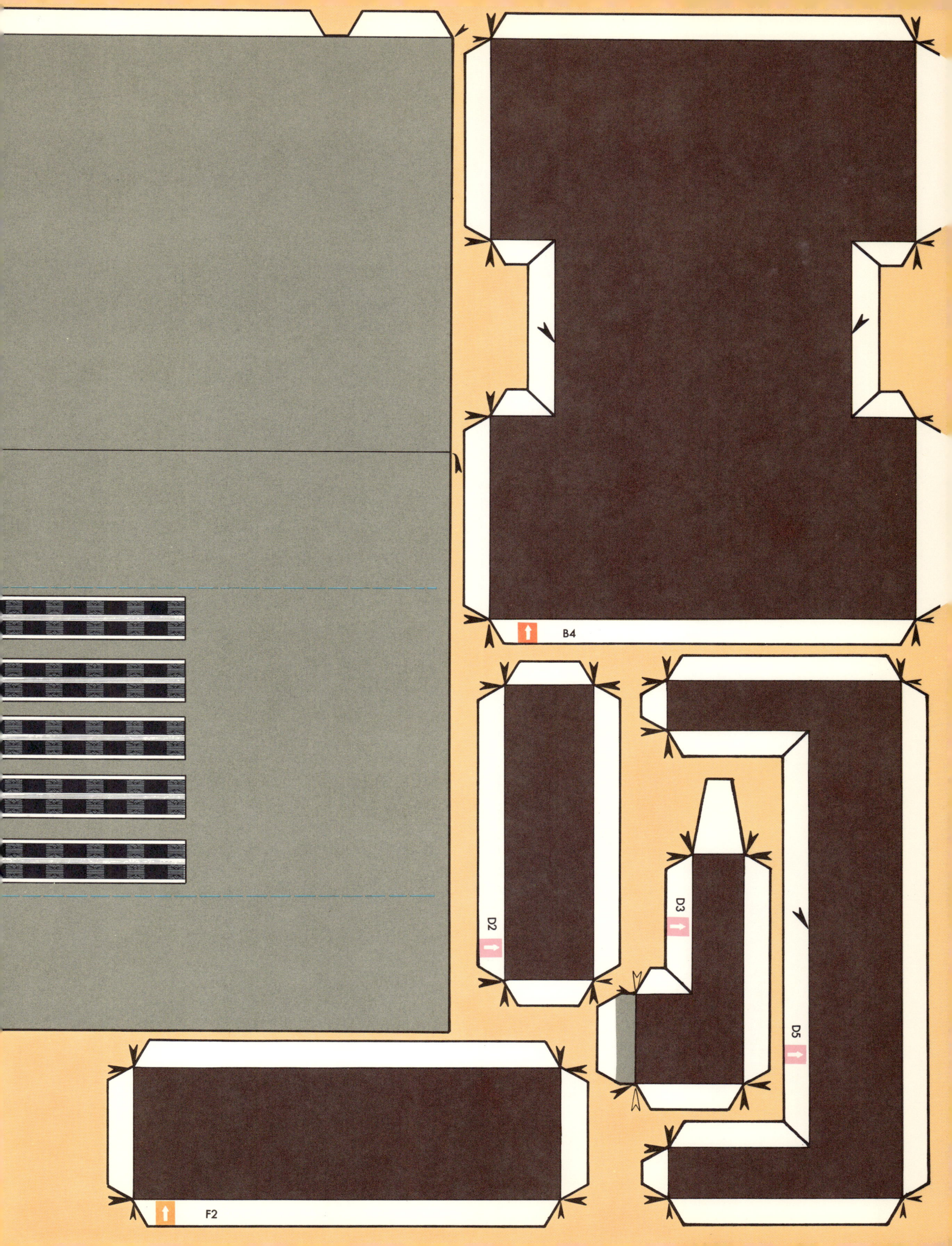

D2
D3
D5

F2

EMPIRE STATE

J3
G3
P2
P3
K3

R1

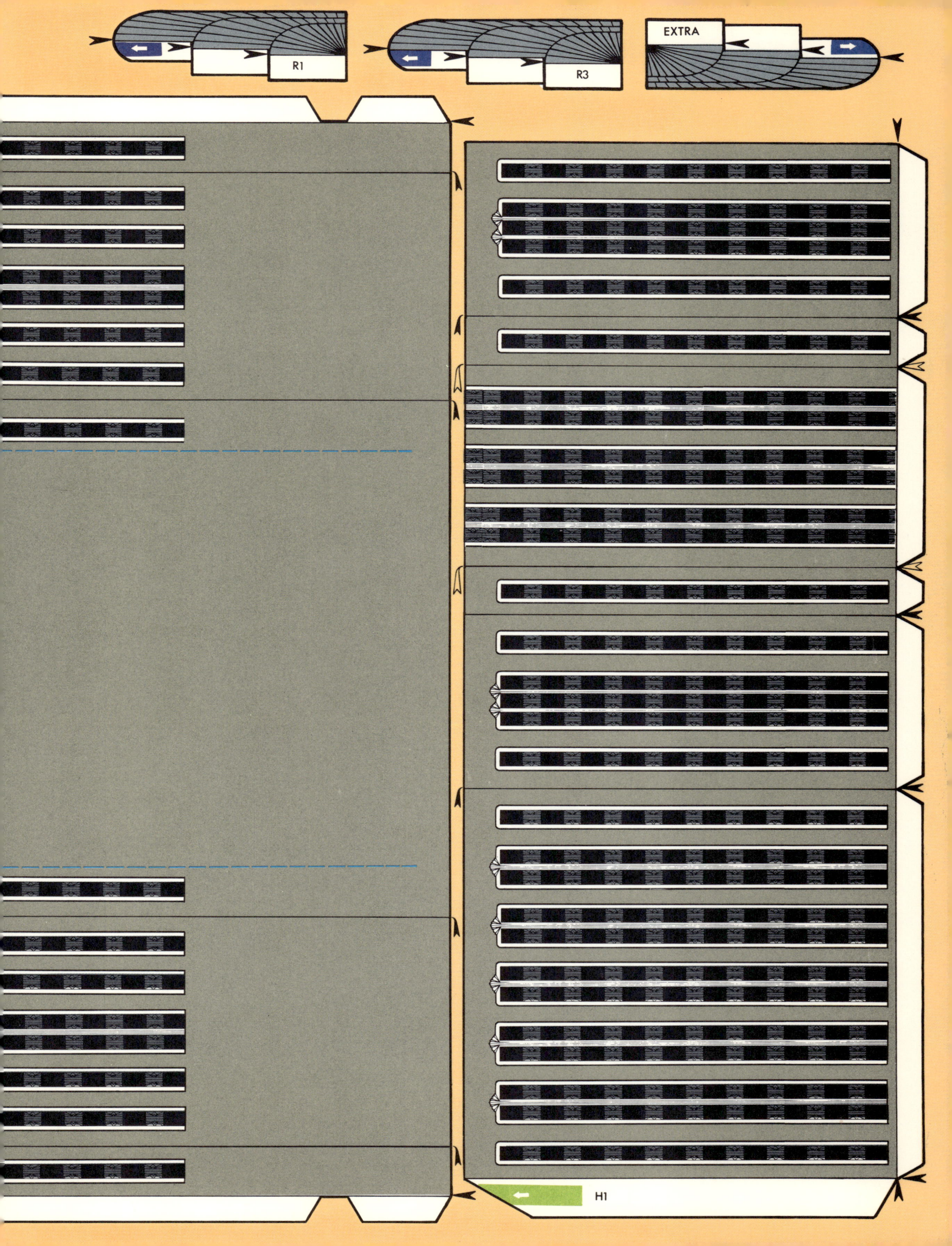

R3

EXTRA

H1

B3

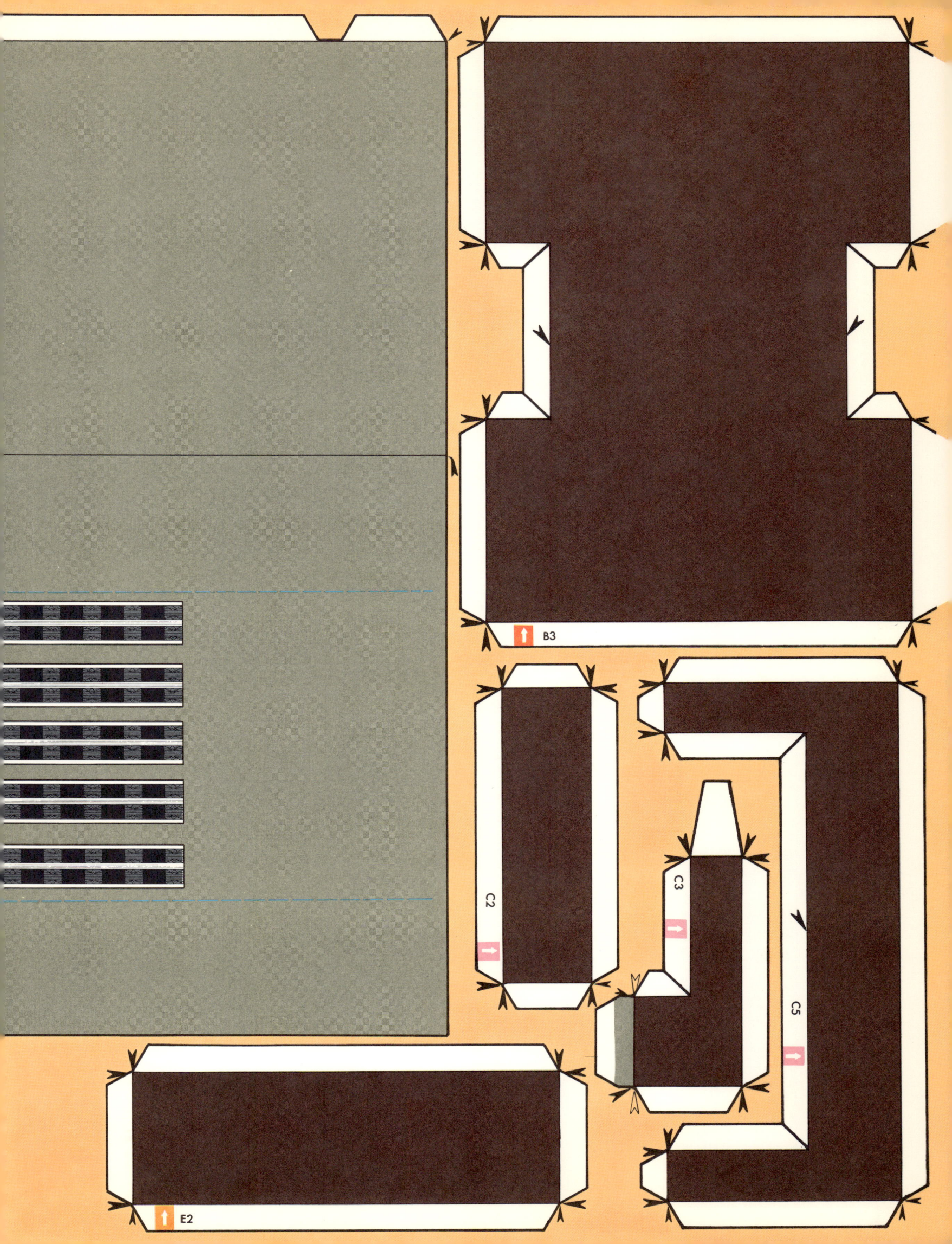

C2
C3
C5

E2

National Car Rental

NATIONAL CAR RENTAL LOCAL DIRECTORY

NEW YORK - LA GUARDIA
LA GUARDIA AIRPORT
95-10 Ditmars Blvd.
East Elmhurst, N.Y. 11369
(718) 476-5922
Open 24 Hours Daily

NEW YORK - J.F.K./ LONG ISLAND
JOHN F. KENNEDY
INTERNATIONAL AIRPORT 11430
(718) 476-5930
Open 24 Hours Daily

BALDWIN
1985 Grand Ave.

BRIDGEHAMPTON
Corrigan Gulf Station
Montauk Highway

EAST HAMPTON
150 North Main St.

HICKSVILLE
235 S. Broadway

HUNTINGTON STATION
379 E. Jericho Tpk.

MONTAUK
Captains Marina
East Lake Dr.

NEW HYDE PARK
N.W. Corner Union Tpk.
& New Hyde Park Rd.

PORT JEFFERSON STATION
4935 Nesconset Hwy.

SEAFORD
4066 Merrick Rd.

SMITHTOWN
157 West Main St.

WEST HEMPSTEAD
580 Hempstead Tpk.

MANHATTAN
305 E. 80th St. 10021
(212) 476-5878
Mon.- Thurs. & Holidays
7:00 AM - 11:00 PM
Fri.-Sun. Open 24 Hours
252 W. 40th St. 10018
(212) 476-5874
7:00 AM - 11:00 PM Daily
PIER 26
Beach & West Street
(212) 476-5896
7:00 AM - 7:00 PM Mon.-Fri.

NEWARK AIRPORT
NEWARK INT'L. AIRPORT 07114
(201) 961-5550
Open 24 Hours Daily

NEWARK DOWNTOWN/NEW JERSEY
975 Raymond Blvd. 07105
(201) 589-8660
Mon.-Fri. 7:30 AM - 7:00 PM
Sat.-Sun. 8:00 AM - 4:00 PM
Closed Holidays

BEDMINSTER
Rts. 202 & 206

1 SELIN
473 Route 27

LAKEWOOD
219 Main Street

LIVINGSTON
111 E. Mt. Pleasant Ave.

MONTCLAIR
120 Watchung Ave.

MONVALE
Chestnut Ridge Rd. & Summit Ave.

MORRISTOWN
168 Morris St.

PARAMUS
W. 120 Century Rd.

PISCATAWAY
443 S. Washington Ave.

POINT PLEASANT
601 Richmond Ave.

PRINCETON
Rt. 1 & Princeton Circle

ROCK AWAY
Green Pond Rd.

SOMERSET
1701 Campus Dr.

SOMERVILLE
Corner Park Ave. & E. Main St.

TOMS RIVER
Rt. 37 E. Westend Ave.

WAYNE
2122 Hamburg Tpk.

WESTWOOD
120 Woodland Ave.

CONNECTICUT
STAMFORD
26 Federal St. 06901
(203) 357-7808
Mon.-Fri. 7:30 AM - 6:00 PM
Sat.-Sun. 8:30 AM - 3:30 PM
Closed Holidays

DANBURY
10 Sugar Hollow Rd.

DARIEN
669 Post Rd.

FAIRFIELD
2424 Blackrock Turnpike

GREENWICH
Railroad Ave. & Arch St.

NEW CANAAN
272 Elm St.

RIDGEFIELD
108 Danbury Rd.

WESTPORT
7 Taylor Place

MONTICELLO
361 Broadway

MOUNT KISCO
271 N. Bedford Rd.

RYE
North & Theodore Framd Ave.

NEW ROCHELLE
635 Main St.

NATIONAL CAR RENTAL EXCLUSIVE
Amoco Motor Club
24-Hour Emergency Road Service

No one has a better reputation for keeping cars in top condition than National. But we want to be certain that your rental is hassle-free. That's why National has joined forces with Amoco Motor Club, one of the world's largest full-service motor clubs, to offer you emergency road service any time of the day or night within the continental U.S. If necessary, we can even authorize emergency repairs by phone at any of the more than 6,500 Amoco Motor Club service facilities across the U.S.

We hope you'll never have to use it. But if you do, it's comforting to know that help is just a phone call away. This new emergency road service offers you peace of mind around the clock because you deserve National attention 24 hours a day.

Here's how to get emergency road service:

- See your rental agreement for the phone number of the location where you rented your car. If you need assistance call this number first.
- If there is no answer at the renting location, or if you are not in the same city where you rented your car, call toll-free 800-367-6767.

National Car Rental

You deserve National attention.®

We feature GM cars like this Buick Century.

National Car Rental Presents...

POINTS OF INTEREST

CONNECTICUT
GREENWICH

Bruce Museum south of I-95 Exit 3 in Bruce Park on Steamboat Rd. contains West Indian, American Indian and colonial material and also has a small indoor zoo.

MYSTIC

Mystic Seaport along the Mystic River where the last of the 19th century whaling ships are exhibited. A re-created village shows the homes and shops of a seafaring community. Working demonstrations of shipbuilding, rigging and seamanship are presented. Other demonstrations include whaleboat rowing and sail setting. Steamboat rides on the Mystic River daily in summer.

NEW JERSEY
ATLANTIC CITY

Even if you're not a gambler, a visit to the casinos in Atlantic City is a must! There are nine hotel/casinos in Atlantic City: Harrah's, Caesars, The Golden Nugget, The Claridge, Bally's, Playboy, Resorts International, The Tropicana and The Sands. And construction continues at a record-breaking pace—there will soon be even more luxurious new hotel/casinos.

The casinos of Atlantic City bring distinction to the world of gambling. The big, plush interiors and unparalleled service lend a touch of class to a vacation or a day trip. The casinos abound with games for your every pleasure. Whether you prefer the suspense of Blackjack ("21"), the elegance of Baccarat, the quick pace of Dice or the variety of Roulette, your table is waiting. And take a chance at the Big Six Wheel and the banks of glistening Slot machines.

It's easy to see why so many people return to the thrill of the Atlantic City casino atmosphere. What an experience. When you're in a casino, you witness the gamut of human emotions—shouts of joy, sighs of disbelief, laughs of tension and delight. And visiting makes you a part of it. You'll be caught up in the drama.

So try your luck in the casinos. Have fun.

NEW YORK
ALBANY

State capital, extending northwest along an edge of a plateau to the Mohawk Valley.

State Capitol between State St. and Washington Ave., and Swan and Eagle St. Housed on the second floor east is the New York State Military Museum.

KINGSTON

Senate House and Museum at Clinton and Fair St. The House was destroyed when Kingston was burned in 1777 and the museum has many historic relics and paintings.

MONTAUK

A resort on a peninsula along the south shore of extreme eastern Long Island Montauk Lighthouse stands 85 feet at the point and two oceanside parks provide recreational facilities.

NEW YORK CITY

Rockefeller Center from 47th to 52nd Sts. west of Fifth Ave. is the world's largest privately-owned business and entertainment complex. Its 19 buildings, covering 22 acres, from a striking architectural group. Focal point of the Center is the sunken Plaza, which is used for outdoor dining in summer and ice skating in winter. Changing floral displays ornament the promenade which connects the Plaza with Fifth Ave. Sculpture and murals are widely used throughout the development. All buildings are joined by a network of underground concourses lined with fine shops. There is an excellent view from the **Observation Roof** of the 850-ft. RCA building open 10 am-9 pm from Apr.-Sept.; 10:30 am-7 pm from Oct.-Mar. Adults $2.95, students $2.00, children $1.25. A one-hour **Guided Tour** of the entire development includes a backstage tour of Radio City Music Hall, winding up at the Observation Roof. Adults $3.95, students $3.45, children (7-12) $2.15. Groups start at frequent intervals, 9:45 am-4:45 pm Mon.-Sat. (489-2947).

Bronx Zoo (NY Zoological Park) occupies the southwestern portion of Bronx Park. More than 2900 birds, mammals and reptiles of 1100 species. One of the largest collections in America—the World of Darkness for nocturnal animals, the African Plains where animals are separated from the public only by a moat. Wild Asia habitat seen via the Bengali Express monorail and the Skyfari cable car. Open daily 10 am-5 pm; Sun. and Holidays til 5:30 pm. Admission: Fri.-Mon. adults $2.50, children (2-12) $1.00 Apr.-Oct.; adults $1.25, children 2-12) 50¢ Nov.-Mar. Tues.-Thur. free. (367-1010).

Chinatown in Lower Manhattan is near Chatham Square west of the Bowery. Chinese restaurants and shops line the streets.

Greenwich Village extends from 14th St. s. to Houston St. and Washington Sq. w. to the Hudson River. Famed for its restaurants, curio shops, coffeehouses and nightclubs.

Statue of Liberty National Monument on Liberty Island was presented to the U.S. by France in 1884. An elevator runs to the balcony near the top of the stonework and a spiral stairway leads to the observation platform within the head.

Central Park in Midtown Manhattan runs from 59th to 110th Sts. and from 5th Ave. to Central Park West. 840 acres of wooded and landscaped grounds. Empire State Building at 5th Ave. & 34th St. is one of the world's tallest office buildings.

Metropolitan Museum of Art at 5th and 82nd St. in Upper Manhattan is one of the great museums of the world. It contains large collections of Greek, Roman and Egyptian art and Near Eastern art and antiquities.

Other points of interest include the World Trade Center, Lincoln Center for the Performing Arts, the Stock Exchanges, Rockefeller Center, United Nations Headquarters and Coney Island.

POCONO MOUNTAINS

Only a two hour drive from New York City or Philadelphia. The area consists of about 1,200 square miles of wooded hills and valleys. Some of the most beautiful waterfalls in the East are here.

WEST POINT

U.S. Military Academy is on the west bank of the Hudson River. It was first occupied as a military post during the Revolution. The post is open daily but cadet barracks and academic buildings are closed to the public.

K1

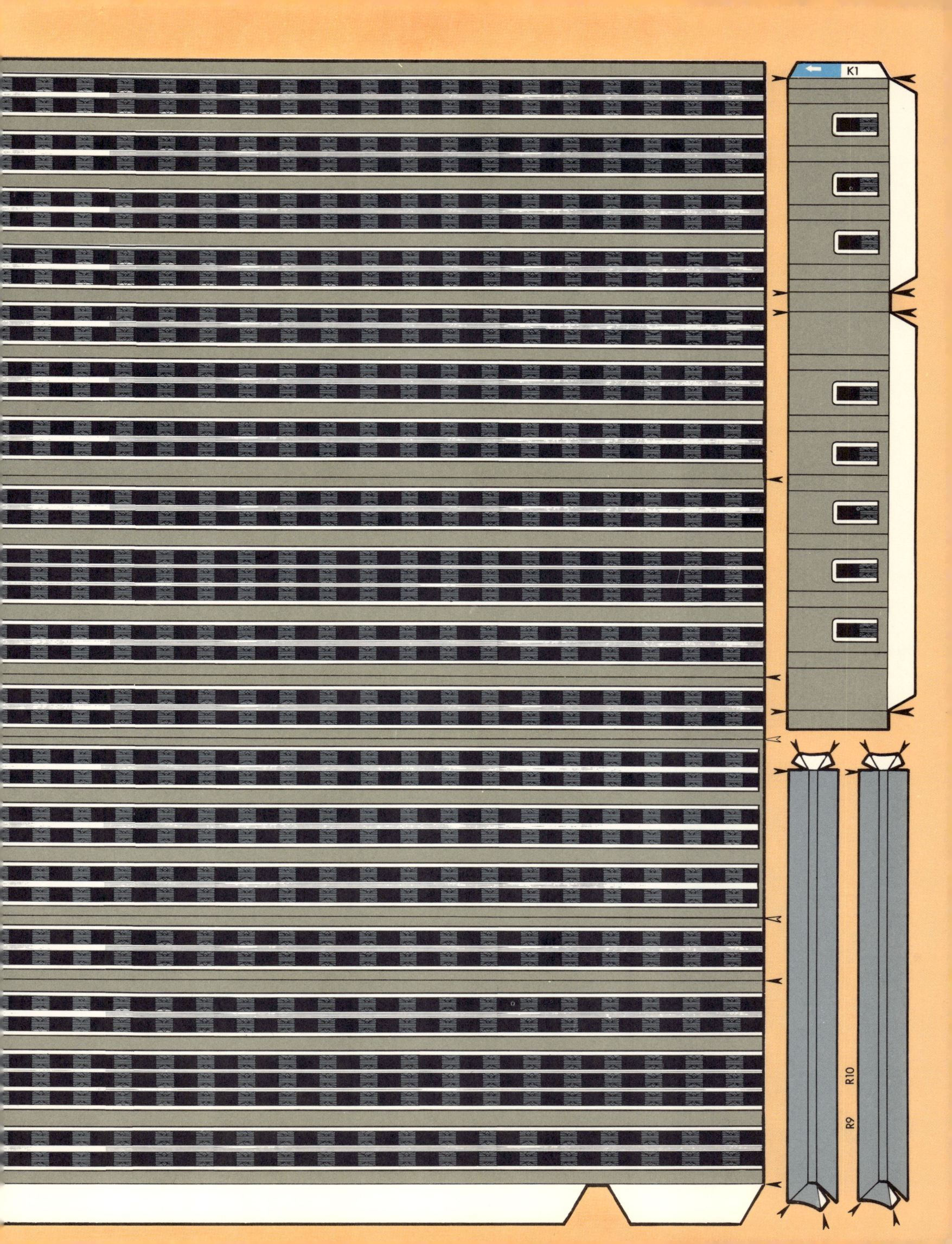

R9 R10

K2

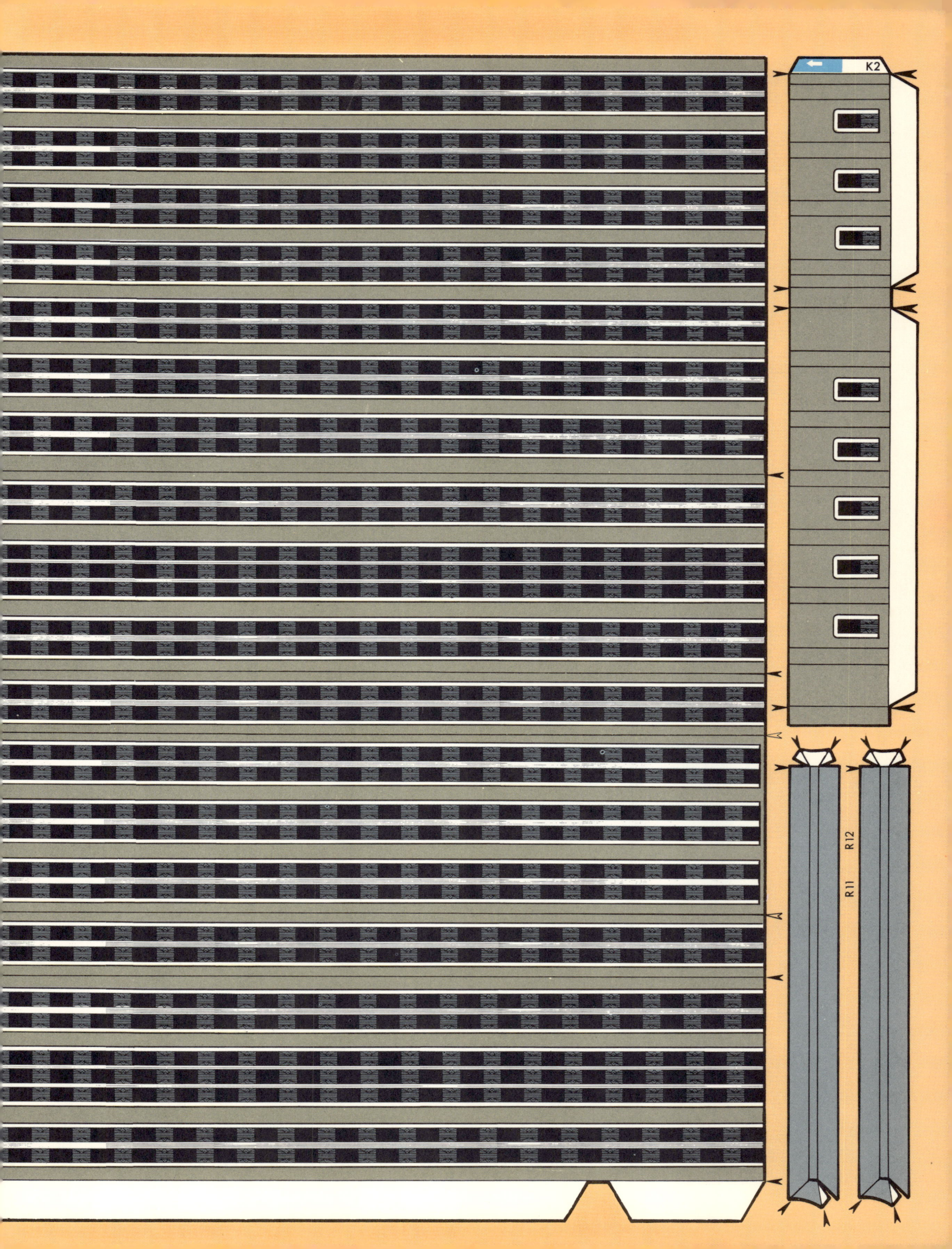

R11 R12

Step 1

Glue wall piece A1 to one **edge of wall piece A2**. Glue support pieces A3 and A4 to the inside of wall piece A1 **approximately 1¼"** from the bottom and approximately 1¾" from the top. The notches on the side tabs indicate correct placement. Now "wrap" the shorter inside walls around the support pieces, gluing them in place as you go. (This "wrap and turn" technique is used often in constructing assemblies similar to this one.) Finally, glue the remaining edge of piece A1 to A2 and set aside to dry.

Step 2

Glue wall piece B1 to one edge of wall piece B2. Glue support piece B3 to the inside of wall piece B1 approximately 1¾" from the bottom. Again, the notches will indicate the right spot. Now glue roof piece B4 to the inside of B1 approximately 1/16" from the top. (To create ledges, all roof pieces are set in approximately 1/16" on this model.) "Wrap" the wall pieces around the support and roof pieces, gluing them in place as you go. Make sure the corners fit tightly. Join the remaining edge of wall piece B1 to B2. Attach the small roof pieces (B5 and B6) to the inside bottom of wall pieces B1 and B2. Allow to dry.

Step 3

Join assembly A to assembly B by applying a thin layer of glue to the tabs on the top of assembly A and to the tabs on the two roof pieces, B5 and B6. Insert the tabs of assembly A *inside* the bottom of assembly B; insert the tabs on B5 and B6 inside the top of assembly A. Make sure the two joined assemblies are straight up and down; if the two assemblies are not in precise alignment, the resulting crookedness will make for a very curious-looking building. Press the assemblies in place by reaching through the inside of assembly A. Set the whole thing aside to dry.

Step 4

Glue roof piece C2 to the inside of wall piece C1 approximately 1/16" from the top. Glue roof pieces C3 and C4 to the inside of piece C1 approximately 1/16" from the top. Glue the support piece (C5) to the inside of C1 approximately 1¼" from the bottom (see notches). Glue support piece C6 to the inside of C1 as illustrated in fig. 4. Set aside to dry.

Step 5

Assembly D is identical to assembly C (step 4) and should be assembled in exactly the same manner (roof piece D2 to the inside of wall piece D1 . . . etc.).

Step 6

Attach assembly C to assembly A by applying a thin layer of glue to all the tab surfaces on assembly C, and fitting C onto A. The blue dotted line on assembly A indicates the precise point of attachment. To make sure the two assemblies align, it's best to do this step with the building vertical on a table top or other flat surface. Make sure support piece C5 is attached to assembly A. You can use masking tape to hold the two assemblies together until the glue dries. Try to keep assembly C from flaring out at the bottom; all the corners should be as close to 90 degrees as possible. Repeat the entire process with assembly D, attaching it to the opposite side of assembly A. Let it all dry. (Don't worry when you see assembly F in the diagram for step 6. You'll come to it in step 8.)

Step 7

Glue roof piece E2 to the inside of wall piece E1 approximately 1/16" from the top. Glue support piece E3 to the inside of E1 approximately 1¼" from the bottom (see notches). Allow to dry thoroughly. Apply a thin layer of glue to all the tab surfaces on assembly E and fit it onto assembly C exactly where indicated by the blue dotted alignment marks. Again, this procedure is best accomplished on a flat surface to make sure the assemblies are flush across the bottom. Hold in place by hand or with tape and allow to dry.

Step 8

Assembly F is identical to assembly E (step 7) and should be constructed in exactly the same manner. Glue assembly F to assembly D as indicated above for assemblies C and E. (See illustration for step 6.)

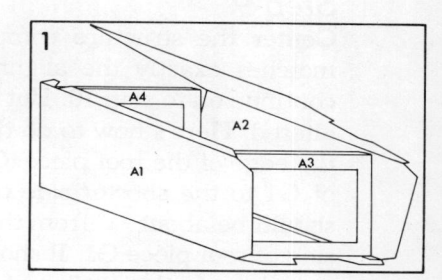

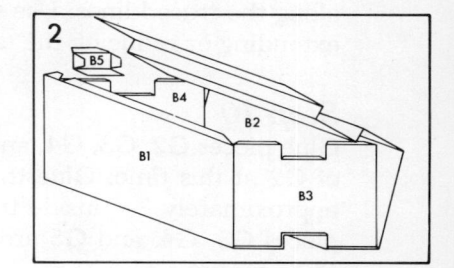

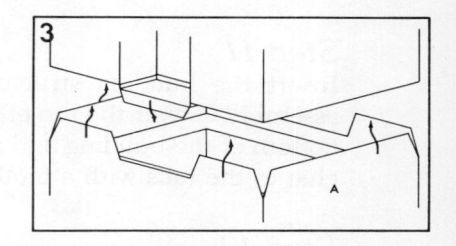

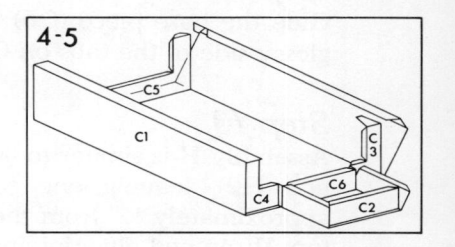

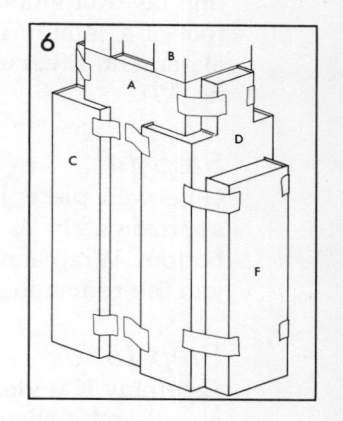

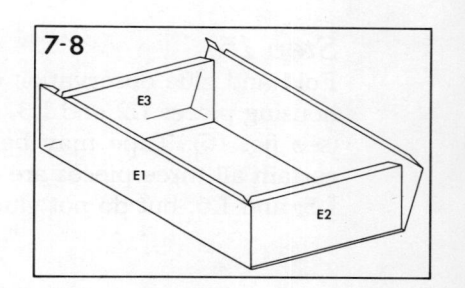

Step 9
Center the structure completed thus far on roof piece G1. If the completed structure matches exactly the alignment marks on roof piece G1, you're in great shape and can continue on to step 10. But if the structure does not align precisely, piece G1 will have to be altered. Here's how to do that: Center the structure on G1 by measuring the distance from the edge of the roof piece (G1) to the side of the structure; the distance from the shorter side of G1 to the shorter side of the structure should be approximately 2⅛" on both sides. It should be about ¾" from the front and back of the longer side of the structure to the longer side of roof piece G1. It should approximate the printed cut and score marks on G1. Using a pencil, trace the outline of the structure onto roof piece G1 (see fig. 9). Now carefully cut along the traced lines. Use the tabs provided on G1, but compensate for your alteration by extending or reducing the tab and score lines. Score after cutting. *Don't glue anything yet.*

Step 10
Glue pieces G2, G3, G4, and G5 together, but do not attach piece G5 to the remaining edge of G2 at this time. Glue the long edge of G2 to a corresponding edge of G1 so that G1 is approximately ¹⁄₁₆" inside the top of G2, creating a ledge. "Wrap" and glue the outer wall pieces G3, G4, and G5 around G1, leaving a ¹⁄₁₆" ledge. Attach pieces G5 and G2 and set aside to dry.

Step 11
Insert the building structure through roof piece G1 by placing the entire street-level assembly G over the top of the building and gently pressing it down and into place until the bottom of the building and assembly G are in alignment on a flat surface (see fig. 11). Apply glue to the tabs with a toothpick or a scrap of paper. Press in place and allow to dry.

Step 12
Glue the base piece (G6) to street-level assembly G. Glue should be applied to the non-glossy side of the tabs on G6. Set aside.

Step 13
Assembly H is similar to assembly B in construction. Glue the two wall pieces together (H1 and H2), leaving one edge unjoined. Glue support piece H4 to the inside of H1 approximately ½" from the bottom, and roof piece H3 to H1 approximately ¹⁄₁₆" from the top. Wrap and glue, joining the remaining edges of H1 and H2 last. Allow to dry. Apply a thin layer of glue to the tabs on the bottom of assembly H and center the assembly on the roof of assembly B. The narrow, recessed walls of assemblies H and B should be in exact alignment. Press in place. A book can be placed atop H to hold it to B until the glue sets (see fig. 17).

Step 14
Glue wall piece J1 to one edge of wall piece J2; glue roof piece J3 to the inside of J1 approximately ¹⁄₁₆" from the top. Glue support piece J4 to the inside of J1 about ½" from the bottom. Wrap and glue wall pieces J1 and J2 around roof piece J3 and support piece J4 and join the remaining edges of J1 and J2 together. Make certain all corners fit tightly. Let dry.

Step 15
Assembly K is identical to assembly J (except that assembly K has no support piece to worry about) and it should be constructed in the same manner.

Step 16
Fold and glue observation deck housing L1. Allow to dry. Fold and glue observation deck housing pieces L2 and L3, and, after they have dried, attach them to the sides of piece L1 (see fig. 16). Tape may be useful in holding the pieces together until the glue dries. Be certain all three pieces are flush on the bottom. Fold and glue observation deck pieces L4, L5, and L6, but do not glue them together.

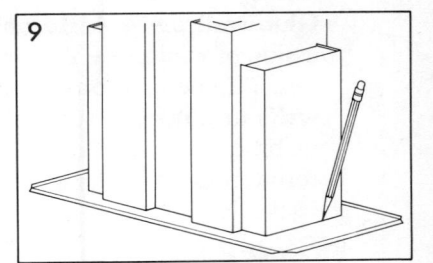

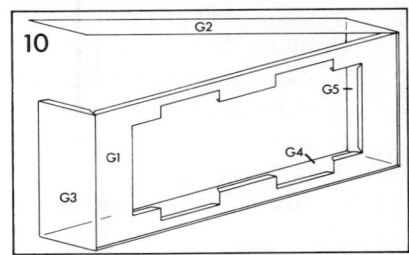

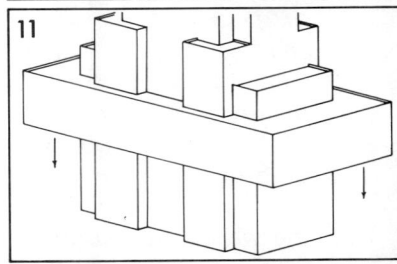

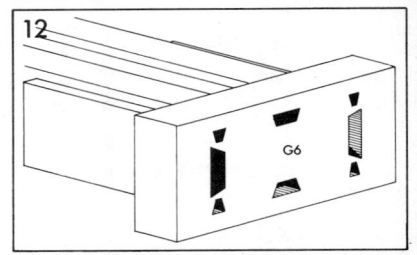

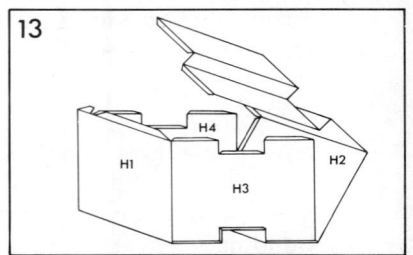

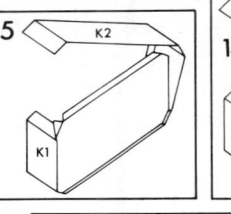

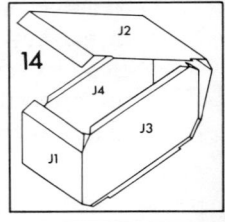

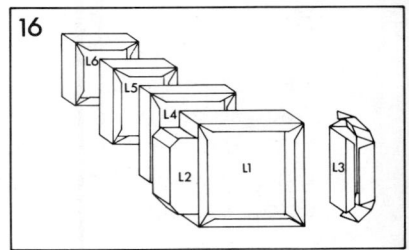

Step 17
Apply a thin layer of glue to the tabs on the bottom of assembly K and press in place in the center of the roof of assembly J. Allow to dry. Mount observation deck housing L1 to the center of the roof of assembly K. Press in place and let dry. Stack piece L4 atop L5 and both atop L6; glue and let set. Place entire assembly on observation deck piece L1. Press in place and let dry. A book may be useful in holding the pieces together until dry. Now you are ready to glue assembly J, K, and L to the top of assembly H. Again, a book may be useful in holding the pieces together until dry.

Step 18
Observation tower piece M1 requires no scoring. Wrap piece M1 around a broomstick or something similar until it is sufficiently pliant. Glue the leading edge to the indicated place (see fig. 18) so that M1 assumes a cylindrical shape. Tape may be helpful in holding the edges together until the glue sets. Next, cut and fold tower roof piece M2 and glue it in place 1/16" inside the top of M1 (a pencil is helpful for maneuvering the piece inside the cylinder). Fold tower support piece M3 and glue it in place flush to the bottom of piece M1. Cut top observation deck piece M4 and, as above with M1, glue it into a cylindrical shape. Mount piece M4 atop piece M3, centered, and allow it to dry. Cut and glue top deck roof M5 and shape it into a cone. Apply a thin layer of glue to the edge of M4 and place M5 on top. Make sure that the hold on piece M5 is square so that the antenna will fit later. Allow to set. Finally, glue the tower assembly M to assembly L. Hold or tape in place until set. Alignment marks are provided where needed.

Step 19
Cut the decorative "wings" with tabs (R1, R2, R3, and R4) and glue to the back of the corresponding pieces without tabs (R5, R6, R7, and R8). It may be helpful to place the folded, assembled pieces in a thick book to ensure the correct shape. Now very carefully fold and glue each of the four braces (R9, R10, R11, and R12) and set them aside to dry. Attach one brace to each corner of the observation tower (see fig. 19), and cover each brace with a decorative "wing." Allow to dry. This step sounds more complicated than it is, so check fig. 19 before commencing. Additional brace and "wing" parts have been provided.

Step 20
Cut, fold, and glue the main antenna structure (P1) and the two upper sections (P2 and P3). Wait for them to dry thoroughly. Press antenna top (P3) into the middle section (P2) after first applying a small amount of glue to the bottom edge of antenna piece P3. Glue P2 and P3 atop the main antenna structure (P1) and allow to dry. Apply a generous amount of glue down the square hole in the tower cone roof (M5) and press assembly P into place through the observation deck tower. Additional antenna parts have been provided. Check alignment closely and hold until dry. If you like, you can stick a straight pin into the top of the antenna.

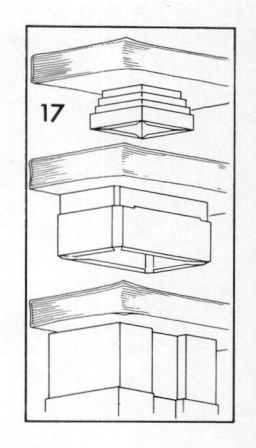

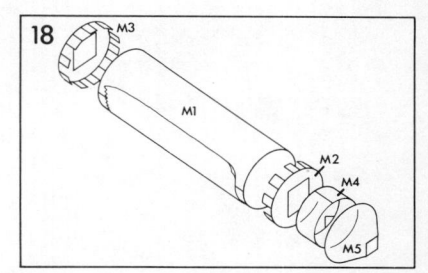

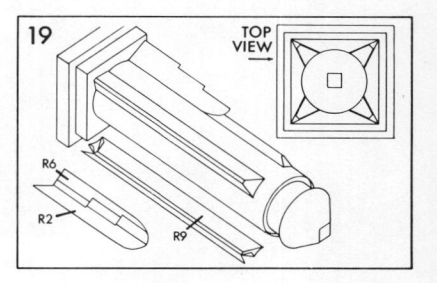

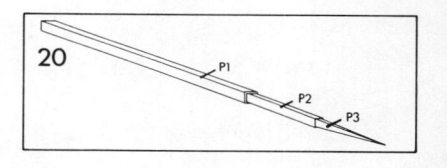

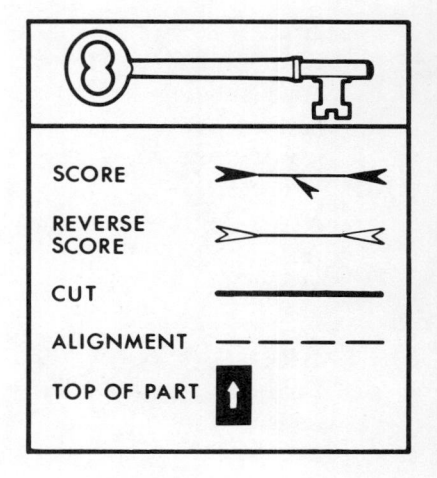

SCORE	>—————<
REVERSE SCORE	>—————<
CUT	———————
ALIGNMENT	— — — —
TOP OF PART	↑